American Moor

Keith Hamilton Cobb

With an introduction by Kim F. Hall

methuen | drama

LONDON • NEW YORK • OXFORD • NEW DELHI • SYDNEY

METHUEN DRAMA
Bloomsbury Publishing Plc
50 Bedford Square, London, WC1B 3DP, UK
1385 Broadway, New York, NY 10018, USA
29 Earlsfort Terrace, Dublin 2, Ireland

BLOOMSBURY, METHUEN DRAMA and the Methuen Drama logo are
trademarks of Bloomsbury Publishing Plc

First published in Great Britain 2020
Reprinted 2020, 2021 (three)

A catalogue record for this book is available from the British Library.

A catalog record for this book is available from the Library of Congress.

ISBN: PB: 978-1-3501-6530-4
ePDF: 978-1-3501-6531-1
eBook: 978-1-3501-6532-8

Series: Modern Plays

Typeset by Mark Heslington Ltd, Scarborough, North Yorkshire
Printed and bound in Great Britain

To find out more about our authors and books visit
www.bloomsbury.com and sign up for our newsletters.

Contents

American Moor debuted off-Broadway at Manhattan's Cherry Lane Theatre on September 8th, 2019. Directed by Kim Weild. It was produced by Red Bull Theater in association with Evangeline Morphos, Elizabeth Ireland McCann, Tom Shea, and Frederick M. Zollo. Set Design, Wilson Chin. Lighting design, Alan C. Edwards. Sound design, Christian Frederickson. Costume design, Dede Ayite. Production Stage Manager, Caleb Spivey.

An Actor: Keith Hamilton Cobb
A Director: Josh Tyson

It was produced at the Robert J. Orchard Theatre, Paramount Center for the Arts, Boston, on April 10th, 2019, by ArtsEmerson (Artistic Director, David Dower and Executive Director, David C. Howse). Directed by Kim Weild. Set Design, Wilson Chin. Lighting design, Alan C. Edwards. Sound design, Christian Frederickson. Production Stage Manager, Tareena D. Darbe.

An Actor: Keith Hamilton Cobb
A Director: Josh Tyson

It was produced at Anacostia Playhouse, Washington, D.C. (Executive Director, Adele Robey) on January 11th, 2019. Directed by Kim Weild. Lighting design, John D. Alexander. Technical Direction, Demetrius Cole Jr.. Production Stage Manager, Gillian Lelchuk.

An Actor: Keith Hamilton Cobb
A Director: Josh Tyson

It had its Boston debut at The Plaza Theatre, Boston Center for the Arts on July 19th, 2017, produced by Phoenix Theatre Ensemble (Artistic Director, Elise Stone and

Producing Artistic Director, Craig Smith) and O.W.I.
(Bureau of Theatre), (Artistic Director, Pete Riesenberg).
Directed by Kim Weild. Production Stage Manager, Caleb
Spivey.

An Actor: Keith Hamilton Cobb
A Director: Matt Arnold

It was showcased in New York at The Wild Project, April
4th, 2015, produced by Phoenix Theatre Ensemble (Artistic
Director, Elise Stone and Producing Artistic Director, Craig
Smith). Directed by Paul Kwame Johnson. Lighting design,
Tsubasa Kamei. Production Stage Manager, Mark
Brystowski.

An Actor: Keith Hamilton Cobb
A Director: Josh Tyson

Biography

Keith Hamilton Cobb is an actor who has been drawn mostly to the stage in his working life, but is also recognized for several unique character portrayals he has created for television.

He is a graduate of New York University's Tisch School of the Arts with a BFA in acting.

Facebook: @KeithHamiltonCobb @AmericanMoor
Twitter: @KeithHamCobb @AmericanMoor
Instagram: @khc_americanmoor
Email: keith@americanmoor.com
KeithHamiltonCobb.com AmericanMoor.com

Acknowledgments

This composition in its present form would not have been possible without the minds, hearts and good faith of all of the following people, to whom I am ever grateful:

Brent Buell
Paul Kwame Johnson
Dr. Frank Madden
Craig Alan Edwards
Gary Sloan
Kevin E. Taylor
Pamela B. Daniels
Arianna Knapp
Craig Wallace
Sylvia DeKnight
Charlie Acker
Katherine Daniels
Andrea Gary
Karen Ippolito
Cheryl Katz
Luna Stage Company
Craig Smith
Elise Stone
Phoenix Theatre Ensemble
Adele Robey
Anacostia Playhouse
Michael Witmore
The Folger Shakespeare Library
Kim F. Hall
Ayanna Thompson
Kim Weild

Introduction

"White producers and directors have quite different perceptions of reality from their black collaborators. This difference alone could lead to casting decisions and conceptual interpretations of the plays, often reached with the best intentions, that are inimical to black interests."

Errol Hill, *Shakespeare in Sable*

Othello is one of Shakespeare's most agonizing audience experiences. There is something unbearable about watching a play with knowledge that could stop the tragedy unfolding in front of you. It is a tension akin to the desperate urgency of the racially conscious subject in a willfully colorblind world. Such urgency propels Keith Hamilton Cobb's *American Moor*, which follows a veteran black actor auditioning to play Shakespeare's Othello for an unseasoned, white director. It is the story of how his blackness and his love of Shakespeare collide with the largely white Shakespeare industry—the teachers, acting coaches, agents, directors (and scholars?)—who subtly maintain ownership over Shakespeare while at the same time insisting that Shakespeare is a universal public good. It is the most discerning and direct confrontation with the racial dynamics of the American stage I have seen in years. It is, nonetheless, hopeful that we can loosen the grip of historical forces that haunt the Anglo-American stage.

Black love of Shakespeare is a site of profound struggle and *Othello* its most vexed object. The rise of Shakespeare as a national poet in the eighteenth century—his "gentrification," if you will—coincided with the denigration of black life in the Americas. Historically, black attempts to stage Shakespeare have been met with the enduring and immensely profitable laughter of the minstrel stage (a global phenomenon with roots in American slavery), when not sabotaged by legal exclusion, racist hostility, and literal violence such as the riots and burning of New York City's African Grove Theater in 1822. Our current era of remembrance and praise of the astonishing careers of renowned actors Ira Aldridge and Paul Robeson can obscure the fact that their Shakespeare performances were weapons in the fight for freedom. For Aldridge, the cause was Abolition, for Robeson, Civil Rights. While now the causes are more multifaceted, the objective of human freedom is no less urgent.

Black performers have a unique relationship to Shakespeare in part because Shakespeare wrote three speaking roles for black men: Aaron, the Prince of Morocco, and Othello. However, *Othello* more than any other play, seemingly offers a place of entry: who better than black people to understand the constant sense of judgment, the suspicion that accompanies being an outsider? Who better to feel the story of a black man with a singular relationship to the state, whose gifts of eloquence and military prowess let him temporarily cross the boundaries of an insular world? Othello's call to have his unmediated story told, "Speak of me as I am," can resonate powerfully for black diasporic peoples who are far too often the subject of others' speech. *American Moor* answers this call by transporting Othello to the twenty-first century in order to explore the outsider status of the black man in Western theater and in Western culture at large.

In traditional productions of *Othello*, the overall vision for the staging is mostly in the hands of white creators and performed for predominantly white audiences. Thus, even apart from the play's emotional extremes, playing Othello makes extraordinary psychic demands upon black actors. It is the only one amongst Shakespeare's eponymous tragedies in which the villain has almost as many lines as the tragic hero. Often, then, *Othello* becomes Iago's play and in many current productions, it's hard to tell whether audiences eventually feel complicit in Iago's laughter or are untouched, sharing his position of white omniscience. We are told that much of the controversy over *Othello* springs from the interracial romance with its striking visual of a black man embracing and ultimately killing a white woman on stage. That performance barrier removed—and with

American Moor's help—we can see the deeper structures of power and the "tyrant custom" that bars full black participation even with a role that "has been more or less wholly the province of large Black men."

Cobb trusts us enough to show in intimate detail the process of inhabiting a character that both was and was not created for you. *American Moor* deftly weaves the complications of the history Shakespeare's *Othello* helped create with the power dynamics of theater. We are all auditioning, this play reminds us, often for roles that fulfill other's needs and other's expectations. Increasingly, we are selling and branding ourselves in hopes of being seen and heard, hired, and loved. The play opens up the audition space where actors brings into action their instrument and their finely honed skills. This space of need and potential is, however, fraught with unspoken expectations, especially around race and difference. The actor must be compelling and beguiling, be thick-skinned and able to take direction and criticism. But a director controls the reality in the room: what happens when your years of experience and skill are unexpectedly and unintentionally turned to your negation? How do you handle situations when the power of your role (or indeed your very being), is turned to "obeisance" and inimical to black interests? After so many encounters, how do you keep your love of theater from turning to dust?

On this note, *American Moor* is as exuberantly hopeful as it is deeply critical. It is a play with uncommon faith in us. As the audience, we are simultaneously the Director, the Venetian Senate, and ourselves: we can stop the racism in theater and in our lives, if we can make the space and time for learning and listening. We don't have to passively play roles as others imagine them. What's past need not be prologue. With effort, we can undo and redo the Shakespeare scripts, the scripts about Shakespeare that we have inherited, and the scripts of Anglo-American life. Cobb gives us glimpses of, not just a different Othello, but of a new relationship to Shakespeare.

American Moor

Speak of me as I am; nothing extenuate,
Nor set down aught in malice . . .

Othello

Characters

An Actor, *African-American, 45–55.*

A Director, *White male, 28–38.*

Place: An American stage in an American theater on an American street in an American town.

Time: Even now, now, very now . . .

A note regarding staging and stage directions

This is a play that requires the sole character on stage to address several different amorphous entities, some that are not physically present, and an audience, another amorphous entity, that very much is. Some instruction regarding when to address whom will be obvious in the text. Other of it is explicitly stated in the stage directions. But much must remain the discovery of the actor and director from production to production, influenced by stage and seating configurations, lighting, and other non-static factors from one production to the next. In this discovery, the audience should and will find itself playing many parts. It is not intended that this process leave them in comfort. But throughout, the actor must return to them often with love and an open heart. He must return to engage them as travelers on this road with him, because that is what, in deigning to sit and experience *this* play, they have agreed to be . . . most of them. The actor asks early on that they trust him, perhaps not with words but by confiding in them. If his tale is to be heard and, more important, believed, he must take responsibility for their trust. This does not mean that he should mitigate any of his well-earned emotional expression, for what would he be without it? His audience will most clearly see his regard and responsibility *for* them in the ways that he returns *to* them.

KHC

*As the audience enters, the Black
actor is sitting, standing, or leaning
against something somewhere on an
"empty" stage. It is empty in that it
is unfinished and un-full, yet it is
strewn with the detritus more or less
common to most theater spaces
between productions. Somewhere
down right facing three-quarters in
is a single chair. Somewhere else the
actor is amongst all of it, and actively
waiting. He "prepares," moves,
stands, stretches, sits again, perhaps
recites, or mumbles . . . but mostly he
waits . . . Always he waits. From time
to time he checks his watch . . . the
way one might if perhaps an
appointment had been scheduled for
noon and it is now 12:20 . . . He
looks to be about middle-middle age.
He holds a worn paperback text of
Shakespeare's* Othello. *(The title of
the play should be clearly legible from
a considerable distance.) Most often
throughout the play he will treat it
with reverence. He is a tall man,
powerfully built and handsome, and
only imposing if you see him that way.
His black, button-front, short-sleeve
shirt with sleeves rolled up over his
biceps is tailored to fit his torso like an
officer's dress shirt and is tucked in
at the waist of khaki "chino" pants
cinched by a plain black, leather belt,
all giving the appearance of a casual
but somewhat militaristic uniform.
But on his feet he sports a pair of
black, high-top sneakers. As house*

> *lights dim, he can be heard*
> *articulating a section of Othello's*
> *speech to the senate, somewhat under*
> *his breath perhaps, but audible,*
> *referring to the text now and again.*
> *Intermittently but perpetually, he*
> *massages and stretches his right*
> *shoulder. And he waits . . .*

Actor   *. . . This to hear*
Would Desdemona seriously incline:
But still the house-affairs would draw her thence:
Which ever as she could with haste dispatch,
She'd come again, and with a greedy ear
Devour up my discourse: which I observing,
Took once a pliant hour, and found good means
To draw from her a prayer of earnest heart
That I would all my pilgrimage dilate,
Whereof by parcels she had something heard,
But not intentively: I did consent . . .

> *There's something in this final line for*
> *him. He looks at the text. He says it*
> *again . . .*

. . . I did consent . . .

> *At some point in the contemplation*
> *of this last, the environment, his*
> *shoulder, he slowly becomes aware of*
> *the audience. It is to them that he*
> *begins to speak.*

I was an English major when I first went to school. I loved the words. But then, I saw Shakespeare . . . not in a book, but on a stage. You know, it was never written to be read. It was written to be seen, and heard. And the moment I realized that, I realized that the only thing lacking from what I had been reading was me. Thirty years ago . . . I wanted to be an actor. What I mean to say is, I *was* an actor,

you know, like somebody is gay I am an actor. It was never a
choice. I wasn't a very good one yet, maybe . . . But it was
in me. It *was* me. And I had learned that I wanted to act
Shakespeare. Now, no one had taught me that, but I had
learned it. Like someone learns that they want to fly
planes. Like someone learns that they want to practice
medicine, I had learned it. At the place where I and his
words intersected, I had been presumptuous enough to buy
in to the preposterous notion that I, my intellect, my
instrument, and my crazy-ass African-American emotionality
could serve the words well, *and* be served well by them. I
wasn't taught that. I learned it. I felt him, Shakespeare. Up
until then, with regard to acting, I had known only of
something called "The Method," having to do with some old
Russian guy, and Lee Strasberg, and about a bazillion
paychecks for American acting teachers over the last seventy
years. "The Method," I was taught. As I recall, we sat around
a lot being all still and quiet-like waiting for some external
stimulus to enter our bodies and compel us to act. "Acting is
reacting," an early drama teacher of mine was quite fond of
regurgitating incessantly. I wasn't good at it. The exercises
put me to sleep. And I *was* reacting, already. Something that
you may not know, young American men of African descent,
whether they voice it or not, have a great deal of external
stimuli to react to, all the time . . . Then, Willy walked in,
and we were only just acquainted, he, she, it, they and I,
when I realized that *these* characters each had this depthless
reservoir of emotion already roiling around within them,
and whenever they but opened their mouths they couldn't
help but give voice to even the most vile of pronouncements
in the most beautiful of ways . . . things like,

"*Would he were wasted, marrow, bones and all,*
That from his loins no hopeful branch may spring,
To cross me from the golden time I look for!"

How many times have you wanted to say some shit like that
about a motherfucker? And suddenly, I could. Without

apology, with every politically incorrect fiber of my animal self I could say,

"... *he made me mad*
To see him shine so brisk and smell so sweet
And talk so like a waiting-gentlewoman
Of guns and drums and wounds. God save the mark!"

I could say that, as well as anyone, and infused with every ounce of my glorious African-American emotional arrogance, it would sing. And so I was beside myself with excitement when an acting teacher, one of my first, asked us to pick a character from Shakespeare and to prepare a monologue.

I said I'd like to do Titania (the middle "a" pronounced like Vanya), from *A Midsummer Night's Dream*. And he said to me,

"The Fairie Queen?"

I said,

"Yeah, sure."

He said,

"Titania" (the middle "a" pronounced like canyon).

I said,

"Huh?"

"The correct pronunciation ... is Titania."

I said,

"You want I should give you a slap?"

Okay, I didn't really say that. I mean, of course I didn't, right? But I wanted to. I mean, he needed to hear it. I thought it. I mean, what are we talkin', potayto/potahto? Grow up! Which one of us is only twenty-two years old, me or you? Ya dick ... Anyway ...

"Why do you want to do Titania?"

"I don't know, I like what she says."

What I meant was, I felt ***her***. We were talking about the "forgeries of jealousy" speech, right? You know that one? Nature is turned upside down, just like now, tsunamis, global warming, snow in June because Mommy Nature and Daddy Nature are having an angry domestic dispute, and she lays it out: "Because of our abhorrent behavior, everybody, and everything, is fucked." And in guilt, and shame, and anger, and because Daddy don't listen, she opens her mouth, and from forth her very viscera, riding upon this effluvium of some of the sublimest language ever given voice, comes, well, what *should* be said, the absolute truth of the matter: *"These are the forgeries of jealousy!"* Now, I consulted the Oxford English Dictionary, and "jealousy," in an Elizabethan context, meant not only jealousy in love, or envy, but suspicion as well, and fear. "Because we are afraid," she says, "we fight."

". . . And never, since the middle summer's spring,
Met we on hill, in dale, forest or mead,
By paved fountain or by rushy brook,
Or in the beached margent of the sea,
To dance our ringlets to the whistling wind,
But with thy brawls thou hast disturb'd our sport.
Therefore the winds, piping to us in vain,
As in revenge, have suck'd up from the sea
Contagious fogs; which falling in the land
Have every pelting river made so proud
That they have overborne their continents . . ."

"The poetry trips up the best of them."

"The best? Who are they? *You* know . . .? Because, look here, I got me a little theory about the poetry. Now, it seems to *me* that too many of these silly, cerebral fucks who get to do this shit are more interested in starin' downstage and recitin' some poem to the audience like they was deliverin' the fuckin' Gettysburg Address than they are in talkin' to the person standin' on stage with them. The poetry will take care of itself, thank you very much. It has for four hundred and twenty odd years. But only *I* can give the poetry *me*. I got this. I'm a pretty unique and inspired idea my damn self standin' here, yo . . ."

Alright, I didn't actually say none of that either . . . I thought it though . . . It happens like that. It has *always* happened *just* like that. Because, you see, from childhood, something else that I was not taught but that I learned is that people in our American culture, who are not Black like me, they do not respond in the same manner to Black men, like me, raising their voices, even slightly, as they do with one another . . . or even changing tone. They do not respond well to my adamance. And so, as Shakespeare's characters are nothing if not adamant, *if* I say it, out loud, swollen with all of my most honest African-American energies, well, suddenly I *am* Titania, or Hotspur, or Troilus, and my emotion, just as theirs, having built and built, it bursts forth from me in unmitigated, unexpurgated vernacular. And the listener all too often has no place for it, no tools with which to hear it, because, you see, I have broken the fourth wall, and he does not recognize the overflown expression of my emotion as the same simple, cathartic thing that it is for anyone, because he is not in the play. Or at least he thinks he is not. He thinks he's just a guy who lives by these American rules, and he wants me to live by them too. So instead, the world of words that these characters are allowed to traffic in:

The **RHY**thms **OF** ar**TI**cu**LA**ted **JOY**;

The **FREE**dom **OF** e**MO**tio**NAL** re**LEASE** . . .

I keep it all in my head. Until I get to *be* Romeo, or Hamlet, or Titania . . . all of the things that *should* be said . . . that should be *heard* . . . they bang around up there looking for the emergency exit only to find it locked from the outside . . .

"Don't do Titania. Pick something else."

So I said,

"Gallop apace, you fiery-footed steeds,
Towards Phoebus' lodging: such a wagoner
As Phaethon would whip you to the west,
And bring in cloudy night immediately.
Spread thy close curtain, love-performing night,
That runaway's eyes may wink and Romeo
Leap to these arms, untalk'd of and unseen—"

"Pick something you might realistically play! Something befitting your age, and experience!"

"O, what a rogue and peasant slave am I!
Is it not monstrous that this player here,
But in a fiction, in a dream of passion,
Could force his soul so to his own conceit—"

"Hamlet is hardly your experience . . ."

"How the fuck would you know?!" I said . . . started to say, but didn't. Instead I said,

"O, she doth teach the torches to burn bright!
It seems she hangs upon the cheek of night
Like a rich jewel in an Ethiope's ear;
Beauty too rich for use, for earth too dear!
So shows a snowy dove trooping with crows,
As yonder lady o'er her fellows shows."

"You're too old for Romeo . . ."

"You got a suggestion?" I actually said that . . .

"Why don't you try Aaron, the Moor, from *Titus Andronicus*?"

". . . The, Aar, but . . . The villain?"

"Sure. What have you got against villains? Some of his most fascinating characters are . . . Well look at you . . . You're a . . . fascinating character, aren't you? Or how about Morocco, from *Merchant of Venice*? He's not a villain."

"Morocco . . ."

[handwritten margin notes:] expected to play Black characters => implications of color-conscious casting? * Shakespeare has a giant cultural legacy that the portrayal & production of his characters are pervasive towards white groups

"They're both probably about your age . . . And . . . well, now you *would* be playing older, but I might even be interested in having you *try* to do something with—"

> *A disembodied voice interrupts from out of the house. He is actually there somewhere, about two-thirds back and center perhaps. But to the actor he will remain, for all he can see of him, a voice throughout the play. It is omnipresent, answerable to, and impossible to ignore. It always has been.*

Voice   Keith?

> *The* **Actor** *waits to hear the call again, a little unsure he heard it the first time.*

Voice   Keith?

Actor   Yeah!

Voice   You ready?

Actor   Sure . . . Anytime . . .

> *He walks down center with his text in hand and addresses the* **Voice** *and whatever he can discern of a person.*

Director   Great! Nice to see you.

Actor   Thanks. How are you? . . .

Director   Good, thanks. I'm Michael Aaron Miller, the artistic director of The Rep, and the director of the production.

Actor   Mister Miller, hello. It's a pleasure.

Director   Thanks for coming in. It's great to meet you.

Actor   It's great to—

Director   Man! You're tall!

Actor   . . . It's great to meet you as—

Director   How tall *are* you?

Actor   I don't know, about 6'4' on a good day. Thank you for having me in.

Director   Sure. So this is Wendy Bond, the associate artistic director of the theatre . . . And Bill Nichols, my assistant director . . . And Ben Wells, our dramaturg.

Actor   Hello. Pleased to meet all of you.

Director   So . . . The Big O!

> *This is that moment of not knowing*
> ***how*** *to say, even if one's mind could*
> *compose* ***what*** *to say, OR, knowing*
> *precisely what to say while knowing*
> *in precisely the same moment that it*
> *cannot, must not be said.*

Actor   *"What shall Cordelia do? Love, and be silent . . ."*

Director   I'm sorry?

Actor   Uh, yeah! The Big O . . .

Director   Do you have any questions? Anything I can make clearer to you before we start? . . .

> *The* **Actor** *begins to speak in*
> *response, but clearly checks himself.*
> *What follows, it should quickly*
> *become obvious, is that what he is in*
> *fact saying is only within himself . . .*
> *and to whatever portion of the*
> *audience will, or can, listen . . .*
>
> *He puts the book down on the seat of*
> *the chair.*

Actor   And *that* is how it begins.

And it's just better when you guys are a little older. Towards fifty is a bit more tolerable to me. You see, it means you've been around long enough to have had the opportunity to know at least as much about Shakespeare as I do, and yet you're not imitating someone imitating someone who thought they knew the poet personally. You ever get that? The dudes who say things like, "And what Shakespeare was trying to say here is . . ." And you wanna say, "I didn't know you knew him like that, Slick." It never bodes well, they start with that shit. Now, you? What are you, thirty-five, thirty-eight? Honestly, I can't imagine you know much, I mean, about this. Look, that last guy who was in here, ya know, the waiting area is small, the door is thin, we see people come and go . . . Yeah, his voice was deep and shit . . . What are we sayin', any un-notable, inconsequential rube can be Othello so long as he's Black? Listen here to me, no cute little 19–20-somethin'-year-old without major daddy issues is gonna want that dude, I can pretty much guarantee you that. The fella before him was ugly and way too short, just sayin'. I mean we're doin' Othello, right? The warrior . . . Whose ass did that boy look like he was gon' kick *besides* the little white girl? Speakin' a' which, he was kickin' the **ho**ly **liv**in' **shit** **of** the **verse**. Fuckin' Juilliard, I bet . . . Taken as a whole, I really have no idea why they are being considered in the same session with me, thus suggesting very loudly that *you* really have no idea what the fuck you're lookin' at . . .

Now how about that for hubris? . . .

If you *were* a little older there might be better odds you'd have a little less to prove, and thus perhaps some small degree of honesty regarding the absurdity of this situation. I mean how many rooms like this I'm standing in front of some . . . guy . . . And he's as scared shitless of Shakespeare as most people, but he studied with somebody who studied with somebody who was British, so he's runnin' with it, and he's lookin' down his nose at me yammerin' on about, I don't know, contemporary relevance and, uh, caesuras, and what the fuck, instead of talking to the man in front of him about the man in front of him. But honesty is seldom convenient, and, of course, *I* judge *you* unduly. I mean, you could be some sorta prodigy, right, with whom it would be heaven's providence for me to work. But I don't get to audition directors . . . You pick me and we toddle off together to Sheboygan to do *your* show, you don't like what *I* do you can fire me. I'm sorta stuck with the likes a' you, ain't I? So, you'll forgive me, but I gotta assess the facts on the ground here, drawing on my experience as a classical actor—I mean, not for nothin', man, look at the resume. I think I slung a little decent Shakespeare in my day—but also and equally, my *extensive* experience as me, standin' in rooms like this in front of guys like you. While *you*, conversely, draw upon your grossly limited experience regarding *anything* like me, as is evidenced by the presence of those two clowns who just had an audience with you. You are doing Othello. And if they're even in contention, then we should end this broken, one-sided process right here and now, because clearly . . .

Shit . . .

I'm already comin' on like a stiff prick over here, right? Take a breath, Negro. Alright, let me take it by the numbers . . . First up, a little white man is asking me if I have any questions about being a large Black man, enacting the role of a large Black man in a famous Shakespeare play about a large Black man which, for the last fifty, sixty years or so, has been more or less wholly the province of large Black men . . .

No . . . I ain't got no questions . . . But you should. You ought'a have nothin' but questions, and yet, you know what?

I'll bet the most pressing question he had for me was, "How tall *are* you?".

> *Retrieving his book, he is ready to begin his audition.*

No, Mr. Miller, I have no questions. But if there is anything that you would like to tell me I am completely prepared to listen.

Director   Okay, well, look . . . Just briefly, in terms of where I'd like to go with this, I'm fascinated with this idea of irrational jealousy. You might recall the story in the news several years ago about that astronaut who completely destroyed her own career by harassing her lover's other lover. Do you remember that? She had driven across the country in an adult diaper to keep from having to stop so that she could confront this other woman? . . . And she was caught, and criminally charged, expelled from the astronaut corps. This brilliant woman . . .   Right? . . . And yet an utter abdication of self-control. Yes? . . . That story stayed with me, that these aberrations of jealousy are phenomena that we cannot justify through understanding. A very old archetype of our nature, of our humanity, yes? *And, what Shakespeare was trying to say here is* perhaps, well, just simply that . . . ". . . *jealous for they are jealous*," as Emilia says, yes? So try to remain open to that as you work . . . I hope that makes some general sense . . .

Actor   Prodigious and powerful Black man . . . ridiculous, petty, neurotic white people . . . in diapers . . . The analogy is strikingly clear . . .

Director   Anyway, let's just do it, and then let's see where we go from there.

> *The* **Actor** *turns and goes upstage*
> *far enough to give himself room to*
> *enter the scene. Then he enters,*
> *unhurriedly, surveying the room. In*
> *the following speech both he, and the*
> *character he enacts, exhibit a self-*
> *assurance that never boils over into*
> *arrogance or bravado. If anything,*
> *until he is moved by his emotion with*
> *regard to matters of Desdemona—and*

even that emotion governed by a self-
determined sense of restraint—it is
rather dispassionate; somewhere
between boredom and annoyance,
resignation and resentment, and
perhaps a private amusement. But he
is relating facts. Othello is always the
largest, most obvious thing in any
room. He never needs to play big,
loud, or self-important.

Actor   *Her father loved me; oft invited me;*
Still question'd me the story of my life,
From year to year, the battles, sieges, fortunes,
That I have passed.
I ran it through, even from my boyish days,
To the very moment that he bade me tell it;
Wherein I spake of most disastrous chances,
Of moving accidents by flood and field
Of hair-breadth scapes i' the imminent deadly breach,
Of being taken by the insolent foe
And sold to slavery, of my redemption thence
And portance in my travels' history:
Wherein of antres vast and deserts idle,
Rough quarries, rocks and hills whose heads touch heaven
It was my hint to speak,—such was the process;
And of the Cannibals that each other eat,
The Anthropophagi and men whose heads
Do grow beneath their shoulders. This to hear
Would Desdemona seriously incline:
But still the house-affairs would draw her thence:
Which ever as she could with haste dispatch,
She'd come again, and with a greedy ear
Devour up my discourse: which I observing,
Took once a pliant hour, and found good means
To draw from her a prayer of earnest heart
That I would all my pilgrimage dilate,
Whereof by parcels she had something heard,

But not intentively: I did consent,
And often did beguile her of her tears,
When I did speak of some distressful stroke
That my youth suffer'd. My story being done,
She gave me for my pains a world of sighs:
She swore, in faith, 'twas strange, 'twas passing strange,
'Twas pitiful, 'twas wondrous pitiful:
She wish'd she had not heard it, yet she wish'd
That heaven had made her such a man: she thank'd me,
And bade me, if I had a friend that loved her,
I should but teach him how to tell my story.
And that would woo her. Upon this hint I spake:
She loved me for the dangers I had pass'd,
And I loved her that she did pity them.
This only is the witchcraft I have used:
Here comes the lady; let her witness it.

Director   That's great . . . Thank you . . .

Actor   Thank *you* . . .

Director   So, I'm gonna ask you to do it again, and this time, ya know, Shakespeare gives us the sense that Othello is also this amazing story teller . . . Right? He has the ability to keep people rapt with these magnificent tales that he tells. And, in this moment, the stakes are really quite high . . . Yes? . . . He's been accused by the senator, Brabantio, of absconding with his daughter, and I would suspect that the consequences for such a crime, if proven, or perhaps even if not, might be rather dire . . . Right?

Actor   Dire?

Director   In terms of the stakes . . . Ruinous, potentially, yes?

> *Again, the* **Actor** *makes the slight*
> *cross to the chair to put down his book.*

And he really needs to charm this senate with this gift of oratory and tale-weaving that he has in order to prevail. So,

let me see him ingratiate himself a little more to them, I
mean, the senate thrives on . . . uh . . . obeisance . . . Right?
Then, when he speaks of Desdemona . . . See, I think the
size of that obsession needs to be set up from the very
beginning in order for it to be a driver in the play . . . Then,
really see if you can win them with these harrowing stories
you tell. Isn't it the Duke that says . . . yeah, he has that line
to Brabantio, "*I think this tale would win my daughter too.*"
So try that.

Actor   . . . Put on your poker face, Brotha . . .

You think that he thinks that he needs to do . . . "a number"
for these guys, in order to succeed in getting from them the
thing that *you* think he wants . . . And so, in order to get this
gig, ah no wait! . . . in order to succeed in getting from *you*
the thing that *you* think *I* want . . . you're implying that *I*
need to do "a number . . ." for *you* . . . It's brilliant. You're
sittin' there, lookin' expectantly at me, thinkin' we're
speaking the same language. But you wouldn't understand a
single word of all that's *not* being said . . . if I said it . . . if
Othello said it . . . Gotdammit . . . I know that your
intentions are good, young man, and that this is not your
fault . . . My anger, Othello's anger, the guard dog, forever
snarling at his chain's end, sooner to strangle himself than
acquiesce to your energy, he does not see you. He sees all the
hovering forces in this room, in that senate chamber, in the
world that have *made* you you, as they are all the self-same
forces that have never allowed me to be me. I'm sorry . . .
You stand in for so much, but I do too, and I cannot just be
me, for you are never, ever, only you.

Breathe, Negro! . . . You're an actor. You're supposed to be
open, available to this "creative process . . ." But, you see, in
matters of race, throughout my American life, whenever
some white person, well-meaning or otherwise, has asked
me to "be open" they have invariably meant, "See it my way."
And in this instance, in *this* play, that is unacceptable. You
think I want to be **your** Othello. And, God bless you, you

have every right to think that. But it's your first mistake. And you're not alone. It's Brabantio's too. Man, I got so much to talk to you about . . . But I've got, what, maybe five minutes up in here . . . and I'm supposed to be tryin' to get a job . . .

> *Retrieving his text once more . . .*

It's nuts, right?

Director   Pardon . . .?

> *The **Actor** shakes his head as if to signify, "Nothing . . ."*

That makes sense to you, yes? . . .

> *The **Actor** nods his head as if to signify, "Yes . . ."*
>
> *He backs up, turns around, wanders a bit, ostensibly preparing to deliver the monologue again. Then with any false bravado and servility he can muster . . . He walks forward. Stops at attention with the stomp of his foot. And he bows before the senate.*

Actor   *Her father loved me; oft invited me;*
Still question'd me the story of my life,
From year to year, the battles, sieges, fortunes,
That I have passed.
I ran it through—Fuck me!! . . . Shit, Sorry,
I'm sorry . . .

Director   You were doing great. You can pick it up right there . . .

Actor   *I ran it through, even from my boyish days,*
To the very moment . . .
Any gift of oratory that he has . . .

> *He tosses the book to the floor.*

Director   Or if you want to start again that's fine too. But I think that's the correct attack on the text. That energy was right.

Actor

> *Dropping the book to the floor
> again . . .*

Right for whom? Right for somebody who thinks he knows how Black guys behave and react? Right for somebody who thinks they know William Shakespeare like they was his therapist? You tell me which one of those you wanna be and I'll take the other, but you can't be both. What is it that will not allow you to let me know somethin' besides how to do what you say? *I* know that Brabantio invited Othello to his house again and again because it was a novelty for him to host the important Black general. I'm sure Colin Powell has had to deal with this sort'a stupid shit too. He's a big deal because he gets to host *the* Black general who's been kickin' Ottoman ass for him all over the Mediterranean. "Let me introduce you to my good friend, *il mio generale, Otello* . . ." *I* know that *Brabantio* liked the stories; that they amused *him*. And *I* know, because I know privileged white guys, that he has no concept whatever that making this majestic warrior run through these party pieces over and over for his dinner guests is like marching out his pet chimpanzee to do tricks. *I* know . . . that it is embarrassing, and offensive, not unlike this distasteful scenario that presently engages us both, as I attempt to keep my little meltdown to myself. "But," *Otello* says to the senators, ". . . *(he)* **still** *questioned me* . . ." He asked me yet again to tell those asinine fuckin' stories about men without heads and other fairy tale shit like that, and then he sat there and laughed in amazement like some simple-minded seven-year-old at the circus. And I ain't stupid. I knew what he wanted from me, so I gave it to him, the more outrageous the better. And now I'm telling you, Senators, that I told *him* the stories. I ain't tellin' *you* the stories. Why the fuck would I *ever* wanna tell'm again unless I gotta

If we're quoting lines here? . . . He says, when he's first brought before the senators, he says,

"*. . . Rude am I in my speech,*
And little bless'd with the soft phrase of peace . . ."

He says,

"*. . . little shall I grace my cause*
In speaking for myself . . ."

Shit, don't *I* know it . . . In other words, "If I tell you mugs what's really on my mind—sans the soft phrase of peace— y'all are gonna get your noses all outta joint and say, 'Oh oh! This nigger's gettin' all obstreperous n' shit.' Any scant communication, is gonna break right down, and I ain't gonna get nothin' done here . . ." He knows his purpose for these men, *and* his value *to* them. The combination of humility and yet the knowledge of one's own worth is called "self-possession." If anything, it breeds composure, stillness, and it too has forever been disquieting to white men when they see Black ones wearing it, so, yes, it is . . . pragmatic for him to "mind his place . . ." He's here to do a job he knows he's damn good at if folks would just get over themselves and let him . . . But meanwhile he stands here, in front of you, having to play this game of civility and field your stupid comments with a look of interest and a smile while wanting nothing so much as to slap you knowing, if he did, that the ages of ancestral animosity accumulated in that single stroke would probably kill you dead. In fact, the most profound thing? . . .

> *Retrieving the book from where he'd*
> *tossed it to the floor . . .*

If you went home and thought for just one minute about how many times today you came this close to gettin' punched in your face by big, angry Black dudes, you'd never do this again.

mollify some other moron who helps write the checks?
Obviously you *potent, grave, and reverend signiors* and I have
got more important business to address, and I wish, for the
love of Alla—I mean Christ, we could get to it. *Il Turco e il suo
drappello non vengono a Cypro per avere espresso e biscotti con te.
Capite?*" You know what that means? "The Turk and his
posse ain't comin' to Cyprus to have coffee and cookies with
y'all, yo . . ." Black, American, and speakin' Italian, that
would confuse the shit outta you wouldn't it? But I do. And
you know what other Black man does? Othello, you stupid
fuck! What other language is he gonna speak in Venice? I'm
givin' ya pearls here . . .

All day long I'm givin' ya pearls if you could hear me . . . if
you could see me, I might just save you from another cookie-
cutter Othello you're ready to run off half-cocked and hand
the public, each time you and every other would-be savior of
the American theatre perennially picks up this play like it
needs you. Like it needs your self-concerned conceptualizing
and your venerated euro-centric scholarship. Like it needs
your huge false set of balls that this American culture gave
you that make you think it's acceptable for you to sit there
on your little, narrow, privileged, lily-white, MFA ass, and
judge a Black man on what a Black man is supposed to be.
"The Big O?" Who says that?!! And what am I supposed to
do when I hear it, jump up and down ejaculating gratitude?
What, did I hit the lottery? Your left-handed scrutiny is no
fuckin' prize. And eventually, some inevitable cataclysm that
comes of this sort of oblivious insensitivity will startle you
out of your stupor of superiority. For Brabantio, it was the
realization that, while he was condescending and laughing
like a half-wit, his daughter was diddlin' herself and
daydreaming about the first opportunity she'd get to climb
on a particular big, stiff, chocolate brown dick. For you? It'll
probably be when some Brotha or another slaps you upside
your head because you are the one pedantic little punk-ass
too many that he's had to stand in front of feigning gratitude
for your ignorance. You're gonna teach me something about

Othello? You're gonna enlighten *me?* Fuck you, white boy!
Shut up and listen. You listen to every last one of us trained
and committed, sacrificin', shit-takin', strugglin' daily
through the bullshit, bone thug thespian brothers walkin' up
in here

> *Again retrieving the book from the*
> *floor . . .*

and tearing off a piece of this play that you couldn't dream
of ever gettin' anywhere near, because our experience so far
surpasses your anemic little awareness on the matter that I
might as well be talkin' to a fuckin' monkey. Watch, and
listen, and *YOU* might learn somethin'. Then, pick the actor
that scares you the most. Because that's what Othello does.
He scares you by being just the opposite of everything you
wanna convince yourself he is, which is the only reason you
give him this bum rap into perpetuity and buy it like gospel,
sayin', "Shakespeare said so." You ain't gotta pick me. But
you're gonna respect that walkin' through that door, purely
by virtue of being born Black in America, I know more about
who this dude is than any graduate program could ever
teach you.

I seem a little angry to you? . . . You think any American
Black man is gonna play Othello without being in touch with
his anger . . . at you? Yeah, well . . . if that's what you think,
then you better go back to having white boys do it . . .

> *There is a re-orienting beat here*
> *wherein suddenly he is not sure what*
> *all has just been said, or more*
> *important, what has been heard.*

I'm sorry. May I just . . . If you would please indulge me, I
would just like to start this again.

Director   Sure, of course.

Actor   Thank you . . .

> *But before he can prepare and begin*
> *again . . .*

Director   In fact, why don't you try starting it sitting, as if everyone is seated before the senate until they've been recognized to speak, then get up into it. See if that gives you anything . . .

> *Reluctantly, he takes the chair and*
> *places it center stage.*

Just for now, let's see if it helps you with the idea that the energy that animates you is so great that it actually pulls you up out of the chair.

> *Reluctantly still, he sits.*

Actor   . . . Michael, I wonder . . .

Director   Yeah?

Actor   I wonder, as an acting point of departure, is it perhaps too laughable an arc to go so precipitously 180 degrees, from huge in one direction to huge in the opposite?

Director   Laughable?

Actor   Is it not the stuff of comedy? Do we not laugh at him come Act Three when he turns on a dime and starts ranting to the rafters on account a' what the white boy, uh, man told him? I worry that we laugh at him. Will it not play better . . . Will it not be better to play, to take him from reserved, even in love, to reserved, even insane?

Director   Well, it *is* the play, that operatic pendulum swing of emotion . . . that attack of utter irrationality that takes us completely away from ourselves . . .

Actor   Yes . . . It is, but, what if, until it occurs, might not the thing that Desdemona is most moved by be Othello's reluctance to put on a face. His sadness, shyness, embarrassment, maybe? Could the "pains" for which she actually gives him that "world of sighs" be those she sees him endure as he rallies a quiet strength to perform that belittling minstrel show yet one more time, most enthralled perhaps with his complete *lack* of incessant bombast?

Director   Minstrel show? Oh, I don't think it's that . . . Nor am I sure why he would be sad, or embarrassed, I mean the man's in love, right?

Actor   Yes. He is.

> *He places the book on the floor by his chair.*

Director   Arguably no more rational a state than the jealousy that follows it . . . What fascinates us is not only the size of the man, but the size of his emotion, his passion the Early Moderns would call it. I think we need to see it.

> *He stares.*

Actor   And you think you're *not* in this play . . .

So what do I do? Do I paint Othello's dignified countenance as a façade which so easily crumbles, turning a great and graceful Black man into a monster, thus suggesting that we are never really that great and graceful at all?

Do I do that for you?

Director   And one more thing. Could you . . . I have this thing about the soft Rs. It always sounds to me like someone attempting to sound British. Could you try and stay aware of that?

> *And what do you say when the very awarenesses and intellect that define your humanity are answered with inanity???*

Actor   . . . Sure . . .

. . . It was called "a Standard American dialect" when I was in school . . .

And ya should'a had me up in front of ya back then, mister directorman, I didn't question things quite so much. I just did it, desirous of approval, beautiful, available, trusting, aspiring, young Black me, while visions of Hamlet danced in my head. Note I did not say Othello. You know why? Because that dumb fuck was the farthest thing from my mind . . . No. Visions of Hamlet, and Prince Hal, and the tear-inducing poetry of Romeo danced in my head, as if the first role that I would be asked to play outside of school wouldn't be one incarnation or another of that same Black boy that Americans of all ethnicities had been so meticulously taught to recognize. And he said things like, "Fuck you, punk-ass, bitch-ass nigga! I'll cut your shit, mothafucka!" The advent of Black urban cinema was upon us. Suddenly "We" had a voice . . . It wasn't mine . . . "But you're an actor," Martin Hoffmann, my first ever agent would say to me. God bless his bald head, he wasn't terribly effectual, ultimately not a lot of clout in the industry, but I believed without a doubt that he believed in me, even if he could never quite wholly understand who it was he was believing in. He was an old-school theatrical agent. What would he have known from somebody like me? To him, any role of any Black male character between 18 and 25 had his boy's name on it. And, at the time, those characters were either the Black sitcom buffoons, or the victim/scoundrels of America's *preferred* African-American reality . . . Not a Hamlet in the lot . . . Or even a Horatio . . . "Yeah, but you're an actor. A good actor . . . You can do anything!!" He believed that for me, and to this day I love him for it. But he could never have understood my lament: "Marty, man, don't nobody wanna buy me as *'anything!'* They only wanna buy me as *one* thing . . ."

Ya know, when you're a tall, Black American male, the one question you get asked more than any other in life is, "Do you play basketball?" Now, when you're a tall, Black American male *actor*, that basketball question comes one question behind, "Are you now, or have you ever been

Othello?" As if the enactment of this pitiful, love-struck Negro who loses his mind over some uncorroborated line of the purest bullshit that some white boy whispers in his ear, and deads his wife is something I should aspire to. Talk of the play for Black male actors begins long before they're actually old enough to play the role. The play's relevance to me was urged perpetually. Older white actors would look me up and down, and then, with a fatherly wink say, "So, have you played him?" no longer even needing to give "Him" a name, but you can bet they weren't talking about Julius Caesar. Others, with no connection whatever to the theatre, would offer unsolicited, "Ah, you're an actor?! You'll make a great Othello one day." And my response, bangin' at the emergency exit from the inside, "What? I'll make a great emotionally unstable misogynist murderer? Why the fu-?!"

But so, I began to read it, and re-read it, see it performed, and to reluctantly contemplate the dubious notion that it *might*, in fact, be a far superior piece of writing than I had dreamt of in my philosophy, and that it *might* indeed deserve to be looked upon as the pinnacle of my classical acting career.

> *He picks up the text and reads from it,*
> *perhaps not quite aloud, but audible.*

". . . *Her name, that was as fresh*
As Dian's visage, is now begrimed and black
As mine own face.—"

> *He hurls the book again to the floor.*

No! No, Gotdammit, no! What brand of credulous, self-loathing baboon, I thought, must such a man be? . . . *And why*?! I was ashamed of him. I was ashamed that any reasonable person could look at me and see him, and I could no sooner portray him than I could show up for one of those Black urban dramas, or some fuckin' dancing monkey coon show sitcom. "Fuck it!" I opined, loudly, raising my voice despite what I had learned. "Look, let me play Richard the

Second if we're gonna get up to shit that ain't real. Because I like him a whole lot better for a whole lot a' reasons than I care for this dumb-ass, embarrassing motherfuckin' Negro!"

> *He is suddenly aware that he is, in some way, public; that he has in fact had a graceless melt-down. The tattered book is on the floor on the other side of the stage testifying to the fact, and people are staring . . . Who has seen it? Has the director seen it, heard it, or just his audience?*

> *He crosses to retrieve his book. He smooths the pages, examining the damage he's done to it. Disquieted by the rage that he has just so involuntarily exhibited, he holds it with reverence again.*

But that was not to remain altogether true . . . You see . . .

> *Gathering the thoughts that will best express this next piece of his story, he sits in the center-stage chair. He has to be careful. Sometimes, there is only one chance to say what needs to be said, and clarity is crucial.*

. . . contrary to the prevalent energies of the *"reasonable"* people that still prey upon the developing perspective of every American Black boy, my sense of self-assessment matured healthily, presided over by the doting ghosts of my brilliant Black progenitors. And then, one day, sitting there dejectedly, on the corner of Me Street and Shakespeare, one of 'm said to me, softly, like in my ear, she said, "Precious baby, that white man whose eyes ya been lookin' at yourself through, he's always gonna need to see certain things whether they're there to be seen or not." And, in that moment, that sacred moment, I suddenly could not *not* care for Othello. I began rather to feel like I have a brother who can't defend himself. And you been slappin' him around for four hundred years. Then, comin' in my face and tryin' to justify your behavior. You're gonna tell me what's *wrong* with him? You're gonna tell me you know his *type*? You're gonna tell me about the family fuckin' resemblance? Well, here I am. You called . . . and not because you was doin' Richard the Second. So now whatchu gonna do? Because now I'm here. And I'm gonna defend and protect this much maligned, misunderstood, mighty character . . . my brother's dignity . . . or maybe my own.

> *A new thought . . . Still careful, he places the book on the floor to focus on making this point.*

*They say of us, actors that is, who know that we are actors first and deeply, that we must harbor the most arrogant of hearts to presume that people would be compelled to sit and consider us with rapt attention upon a stage. But also, that we must harbor the most heroic of hearts in order to weather the endless rejection as we continue to venture forth,

> *The energy of this thought actually does pull him up out of the chair and onto his feet again.*

cleaving stalwartly to that sense of self; to seek distinction in an industry that perpetually tells us, "You are *not* compelling enough. You are *not* good enough. Everything about you is *wrong*."

But one other thing that, as a young Moor, I was not taught, but that I learned . . . Desdemona . . . Lovely, self-possessed, listening, discerning, inconceivably brave, watching. Desdemona is thrilled that such a man even exists. That one of him is actually a thing is a joyous revelation to *her*. Her

---

* See Appendix 1, p. 44.

very being emanates . . . upon seeing him standing there, what is he, he's large, and dashing and dark, yeah sure whatever, how he moves, like nothing she's ever seen, how he stands, sure, fine. Look, so far beyond any of that bullshit . . . is how, beneath a too often scowling brow poorly concealing fifty years of adversity, she can see a child's eyes, and a little boy's thoughts forming behind them, and how his sculpted mouth makes words, and yet they are not always the words that express the thoughts that she sees him thinking . . . How far more often she sees that they are just the things that his situation demands that he say. And as she sits demurely through these congresses of men, her being in silence exclaims,

"I, for the fact that such as you so much
As breathes, am jubilant.
I feel you deeply, great and lovely thing,
In heart, and in my throat, and in my belly."

Because of what they say of us, this American life has never been my game to play. If I try to play it, my only strategy has ever been to attempt to appear less of what I am. But this is a fool's errand, because the thing that I am is so very apparent, and really quite impossible to disguise. And so, though I fit not your equation as seen through your narrow little lens, little shall I grace my cause, Othello's cause, the play's cause, the American theatre's cause, to pretend that I don't know that you are frightened of me.

He returns to the chair and sits.

You are afraid of me. I am afraid that nothing will ever change. And these are the forgeries of jealousy.

Director   Something else?

Actor   Leap and the net will appear . . .

Director   Pardon me?

Actor   Uh . . . Yeah, Michael . . . Before I jump into this
speech again, may I? . . . It is my sense that Othello has been
this essential commodity to the Venetians for some time. And
. . . Uh, well, frankly, he is the *only* large, Black entity in the
room. He is aware that he comes at a premium to these men
of the senate . . . *and* that he is unique . . . Which is to say, I
suspect that if he *whispered* his speech the room would
listen . . .

Director   Hmm?

Actor   Look, might I just suggest that they are not to him as
Brabantio is, but that his strong sense of self informs his
perception that they are already on his side, or at least,
attentive to him regardless of oratorical flare? . . . Uhh . . .
Because they know that not just anyone can play his part,
the extent to which *he* knows they know renders, not
manners, but obsequiousness unnecessary . . . And he
knows, so—

Director   Well yeah, maybe, but *we* know that at least one
senator, Brabantio, isn't motivated by rational attention to
the over-arching needs of the state. How many others might
not be? I mean, let me play the devil's advocate . . . A little
obsequiousness might not be a bad thing.

Actor   **Nobody ever plays the devil's advocate. They play
their own advocate, and hide behind that stupid idiom to
avoid having to take responsibility for it.

Director   You do get that, right?

Actor   Yeah, I get that . . . And now that I've crucified my
every chance of actually getting this gig . . . You wanna play
devil's advocate? Whadya got, Bruh, three weeks? Maybe
four? Ya got three weeks in rehearsal, ya got five minutes
lookin' at me in this room. Othello on the page, or the Black
man standin' right in front of you; in that short space you
can't do nothin' but fucking pretend to understand shit

** See Appendix 2, p. 47.

about either, so . . . why you wanna do this play? I mean, just
to play the devil's advocate . . . Why you wanna punish
yourself with having some big-ass angry Negro all up in your
grill gettin' ready to so ungently disabuse you of all of your
most deeply seated notions about sex and race and religion,
and most important, self? You don't . . . You ain't gonna
confront those notions fully if you rehearse for a year, so
maybe this here five minutes is gonna be just about all your
unimpeachable porcelain perspective can stand. Then,
you're gonna go right on ahead, take whatever you *think* you
know, and ram it greaseless straight up into that three-week
hole whether it fits or not and call it "theatre." Yeah, well,
ouch!! Just to play the devil's advocate . . .

Ya know, if you and I, we picked up a *New York Post*
tomorrow morning, and the headline was some guy put ten,
eleven bullets in his girlfriend, and he said, "I loved her so I
had to kill her . . ." we'd say, "What a fuckin' mook!" Then
we'd throw the paper in the garbage and we'd go have
coffee. We wouldn't stand there sayin', "Hey, let's go do a
play about this sorry, selfish sack a' shit." But let me be clear.
I ain't sayin' that the circumstances motivating the *Post*
shooter *and* Othello can't be damn near legit if you dig deep
enough. This is my point. Down underneath, we're all
getting our fragile human condition smacked around every
gotdamn day, and nobody sees, hears, contemplates, gives a
fuck, until it all comes out somewhere horrible . . . What I'm
sayin', there's stuff there to make a play worthy of four
hundred years, but that ain't the story they've been tellin'
over four centuries, and you can't tell it any better in three
weeks, you can only tell it *again*. And the bigger issue is that's
all you ever really wanna do. How do I know this? Because
the second I even begin to suggest that my Black
consciousness when discussing matters involving Black
characters is a more accurate assessor of truth than yours,
the look on your face says, "Just what are you accusing me
of?" I'm accusing you of not knowing what you couldn't
possibly know and wanting you to just admit that you don't

know it. You'll turn right around and call that "playing the race card." Motherfucker, you're doin' Othello. You picked up the race deck. When your casting director called Black me and asked me to come up in here and be seen by white you for *this* role, you dealt me the race hand . . . What other cards you want me to play? Hold'm or fold'm but you're gonna finish the hand. Then you can take back all the cards and go deal to some other Negro if you want to.

'Cuz there are colleagues of mine who will be all too happy to be **your** Othello. And they'll proudly stamp it on their resumes, right there next to Walter Lee Younger and seven or eight roles by August Wilson. And perhaps they're Black men who are old enough, and wise enough to let you do whatever it is you believe you need to do; journeymen actors, like the Moor is a journeyman soldier, conscientious, resigned, and ready to do the job, take the money, pay a few bills, and get on back to doin', I don't know, *Fences,* for the fifth time in Houston somewhere. But you don't want an actor with an old, tired spirit; one that was long ago just too worn down to push back at your silly, one-sided awarenesses anymore. Do you . . .? Or some slight and ineffectual tradesman to gratefully grumble, seethe, and slap the white girl around at your direction in assurance that the story *you're* telling is told . . . "*I,*" the Moor says, "*. . . I fetch my life and being from men of royal siege . . .*" And he brags like that because the truth is that this proud Prince, at his core, is a boy . . . He is a boy.

> *By this point, he has leapt up onto the seat of the chair. He is frenetic and impetuous . . . like a boy . . . He sits up on the chair back, and speaks with a new intensity. So much to say, so frustrated by the insecurity that anyone can actually hear it, much less understand it . . .*

He is an arrogant, ill-mannered, perfect, precocious Black child in the body of an aging badass. But he is a boy, like Tamir Rice was a boy . . . like Trayvon Martin was a boy, who would challenge you for the right to *his* truth and *his* dreams, because that's what boys do, just as I strain at the bonds of decorum to challenge you now. And if, by some slim odds, this boy can survive the forces perpetually bent upon denying him the unapologizing self-actualization of his beautiful black being he will champion those dreams right on into "*the veil of years.*"

I've got this vision of lifting Desdemona up over my head . . . Like this . . .

> *He leaps from the chair and lifts his arms, first with bent knees, then straightening to full height with his arms extended above him as if lifting another person into the air while holding them at the waist. First to the right . . .*

In life and love,

> *Then to the left . . .*

and in death and despair. So they tell me, they say, "Get a small Desdemona." But I say love knows not from size. What if she's a tall, handsome, big-boned woman, his powerful complement? Then I better hit the gym, because Othello, *my* Othello, could do that. The full focus of his huge, boyish energy could, and would do that regardless of the size of his beloved. For me, such an image is essential. Because it says, "How powerful this man is . . . How full of impetuosity, pathos and play. How joyous and intense to do such a thing," and he . . . and *there*, mister directorman, is your "very old archetype of our nature." The warrior heart, manifesting in every last thing that this man does until the day he dies. Warrior as lover. Warrior as protector. Warrior as clown.

Even warrior as wife murderer and abject disgrace to all that conspired to create him . . . But warrior.

> *He lifts her jubilantly again. First to the right . . .*

In life and love . . .

> *Then, moving to the left, he makes the emotional journey from joy to misery . . .*

> *Slowly, he sinks to his knees, lowering Desdemona's body gently to the floor, where he stays hovering over her in desperation and anguish, ultimately collapsing onto the floor himself.*

> *At length, he collects himself.*

So about a year ago, I start feelin' this shoulder when I'm liftin' heavy stuff. The doctor says, "Eh, you're older. A little arthritis, a little tendonitis . . . Shit's gonna start to break. It can hurt. It's that time." And I say to the doctor, "What about all of my unrealized dreams? . . . I've been struggling after them for so long, so hard, through ugliness and inequity, through false perceptions, pettiness, and the lack of any forum wherein I might even attempt to assuage anonymous fears . . . I've been faithful, and patient . . . I turned around and I was fifty-two . . ." So I went to the gym, it only made it worse. A little Celebrex will help if you wanna risk a heart attack. But it will not allow us to forget that, at the end of the day, we're just old. And, for all of our dreaming, and sincerest of positive intentions, there will be diminishing returns. The Moor knows this. Shit, y'all, *I* know this. But it doesn't make us grow up, does it? It only makes us grow angry.

Othello enters that scene like I just entered this dingy-ass, empty, cold motherfuckin' room, under scrutiny, his boyhood dreams now unrealizable, those of adulthood clearly in jeopardy, and immediately aware that who he *is* is not the *he* either sought or seen by those he stands before. In his heart, he is an invincible, indestructible powerhouse of a boy, with a deep, boyish desire to please, to be praised, to make people proud of him; that fire blazing in his guts that makes him want to woo women and put babies in their bellies, and stand up for principles, and protect others, and create legacies, and earn honor. In his heart, he is Caliph of all Iberia still, and he strides about on his great, stout legs, laughing as big as any sky, and letting his beneficence bathe over all those about him. And he shouts from the shore from the bottom of his voice to the top of his mighty lungs so as they hear him back across the Strait of Gibraltar, in Morocco, Mauritania and back through the ages of his people's glorious past, "Have I not done well? Am I not wonderful, just as you?" *This* is what stands before that senate, his human being seeping out of every pore. And I suspect that amongst them they would say, because I have heard them say it of me, with words and without, "Where does he get his balls so big to act like *everything* that he is?"

***Now, in his head, as he is facile in the assessing of any battle, he can reckon with ease what time and conditions hold in his favor and which do not. And there before the senate, like a fortress on his feet, he holds forth with the hint of a recurring smile. But there within . . .

> *As if age and fatigue have suddenly overwhelmed him, he sinks down into the chair.*

. . . in all of those other once so impregnable places not quite head and not quite heart of a body begun to betray him, he knows he is old . . . He knows he is epileptic . . . He knows by now that no one is going to erect a statue on the Rialto to the memory of the great General Othello, the Moor. What did you call his situation, "dire?" He smiles, compensating for

---

*** See Appendix 3, p. 48.

despair that you have no clue, nor the first genuine concern what is, in fact, dire about his situation. His smile is like an involuntary spasm on the edge of insanity. How does one maintain one's sanity when so much of what one is has forever been held in such strict and unnecessary abeyance by other's fears and the rules that one never agreed to? You want mental fragility, all the tiny little cracks in Othello's armor that might make him finally snap completely and kill someone, even if that someone were the solitary love of his life? Forget women in diapers . . . Forget all that is familiar to you . . . Look at me. Listen to me. I might know . . .

Director   Are you with me?

> *The **Actor**'s response is at best a non-verbal attempt at acknowledgement, but he picks up the book and opens it in preparation to attempt the monologue one more time.*

Great, so, yeah, let's just see you get up into it . . .

> *After a moment of preparation, he rises quickly to his feet. But instead of beginning the speech again . . .*

Actor   . . . Some of my brothers, strong, elegant men, Black and warlike, erudite, and vigilant, have asked me why. They say, "Little Brother, why? Why, why, why, why the broken vessel of Othello, incapable as it is of holding everything that we are; our breadth and depth, our magic, our magnificence; incapable of containing our truth? Why seek vainly to redeem him? He is no kin to you, rather he is the child of one who could have had no love for you. Nor can they who perpetually pick up this broken vessel and attempt to stuff you into its confines, making you fit to *their* satisfaction."

> *He pauses, considering this perspective from this new voice, perhaps as the younger attempting to*

*offer a response to a stern admonition
from the elder . . .*

The truest truth is that I am no Danish Prince either, or
Titania . . . I am only me. I have *only* this to lend to anything.
And I love him . . . not Othello so much, except in that if I
act him, he is me, and I love me dearly. I love Shakespeare.
I love the sound of his voice. I love to hear him speaking
through me. I love him just as I love you, Black man,
for you speak through me too, and you can see all the scant
good *your* noisy-ass, fearsome fuckin' voice has done me in
America . . . And yet I have not sought to disavow *your*
obtrusive energies the way they march before me into
every room . . . I love you both. I wrangle with your rights
and wrongs, your intentions and accomplishments,
I struggle with your improprieties born of old age and
tradition. I admonish loudly your mistakes. I am, by turns,
embarrassed, and inspired . . . emboldened by you both,
two mighty forces converging in me. What does Hamlet say?
". . . *the readiness is all*." Man, I have been ready for some
thirty years to at least attempt his lovers, his warriors, his
fools. And yet to most, I have only ever looked like this one.
And *he* is lover, warrior, and fool all at once. Tragically
flawed, yes . . . Just like you, Brotherman, and like me. Like
everybody. He is wholly human. But *he* is Black. And to be
Black here has only ever meant to be more misread,
misrepresented, misinterpreted . . . more misunderstood.
And maybe, just maybe a little something this poor player
can lend him, and someone, one, anyone will say, "Ah! I see!"

*Self-love, my liege, is not so vile a sin
As self-neglecting . . .*

I can offer you the Moor from the inside out, and, standing
before you, let what *I* feel be everything . . . Then, you will
see whatever you see. And what you feel *about* me will be
everything else. But I remain the intelligent, intuitive,
indomitable, large Black American male actor. And perhaps
the purpose is defeated, but it does not honor God not to

act like *everything* that I am, hoping that you will say, "I see!"
but honoring God regardless. And *there's* our tragic flaw,
Brotherman . . . It's these huge hearts, yours, Othello's, and
mine, that daily endeavor valiantly . . . desperately to believe
in the inherent goodness of *all* men.

> *Retrieving the book one last time from
> the floor . . .*

Not wisely . . .

> *Finding the page . . .*

But too, too well.

> *He comes to attention with the stomp
> of his foot as he did in the previous
> attempt. And he bows before the
> senate . . .*

*Her father loved me; oft invited me;
Still question'd me the story of my life . . .
Still question'd me the story . . .*

> *But inauthenticity is impossible
> now . . . Truth comes in tears, like
> exhaustion, and the closest we
> have seen this warrior to complete
> emotional collapse. Then, as if to
> rally . . . as a warrior would . . .*

. . . You know . . . Michael . . .

Director . . . uh, yes? . . .

Actor The Moor has this line. He says,

*"The tyrant custom, most grave senators,
Hath made the flinty and steel couch of war
My thrice-driven bed of down . . ."*

"It is customary for me to be at war, and so I'm used to it."
Right? Easy . . . But then, by this trick of analogical irony, a
vastly more relevant meaning leaps off the page, this surge

of wrathful, ancestral energy rages through me, and I
cannot shut my mouth. He says, "The tyrant . . ." The thing
by which I have to abide, and "custom . . ." the protocols that
you made up, "*The tyrant custom, most grave senators . . .*" my
having to obey *your* rules has made a war zone my refuge!
And I'm sure the point is completely lost upon them. You,
Michael? I know I must look positively bat-shit crazy to
you standin' in this room frantically struggling to edit out
anything remotely threatening from my speech. But with a
Black actor, a white director, and *this* play there is never
anything out of context. An American Black man burns
a whole lotta calories trying to keep a rein on full *half* of
himself just so people around him don't get nervous. I'm
done. I do not mean to scare you, but I do it just standin'
here, so how may I honestly express to you the joys, the
hurts, the rages that would realistically compel this
character's life without you piss yourself and call me crazy?
You don't want a man, you want a cartoon. Did I ever tell
you how much I suck at basketball? . . . I have finally become
a decent actor though, and I know one hell of a lot more
than you about being the big Black guy in the room.

Director Uh . . . Okay, listen, there is no reason –

Actor No! . . . No . . . For once, for the sake of anything
ever changing just the slightest little fucking bit, *you*
listen!! . . .

> *Having now finally, and flagrantly,*
> *disrespected the invisible line of*
> *protocol, he begins the following, but*
> *it is clear through his movements and*
> *the tone of his voice that he must at*
> *first "forcibly" but without contact*
> *keep the auditioner from responding,*
> *or even attempting to leave the room.*
>
> *As he continues, the director attempts*
> *to interject. Their lines are spoken*
> *over one another in full voice. The*

> *director does not hide the fact that **he**
> knows **his** place.*

Ya know, my mom and pop—

Director   Look, I understand where you're trying to go
with this—

Actor   No, listen, my mom and pop, they do—

Director   and you've got some interesting ideas—

Actor   MY MOM AND POP!!—

Director   But look, this is not the time or place to have this
discussion!!

> *The **Actor** pauses to absorb this last
> final iconic pronouncement. Then . . .*

Actor   . . . God bless you, you're beautiful . . . My mom and
pop, they do this thing for seniors, at a community college.
They go once a week for a month and spend a few hours
learning about somethin'. And you're gonna find, which
seniors have a hundred and fifty disposable bucks to spend
on this sorta thing every so often that doesn't feed, shelter,
or clothe them? Generally, most often? It's white ones . . . So
they can select new topics every few months or so, what they
wanna learn about. So they decided, my mom and pop, that
they were gonna do "The History of the Mafia," and "The
Taliban Phenomenon." So I asked, I said, "Pop, how come
you's didn't wanna do 'Mark Twain's *Adventures of Huckleberry
Finn?*'" My old man, he's eighty some odd years old, you
know what he said, he says, "I don't need to sit and listen to
a bunch of white people discuss Black people with me in the
room." He and I, we've never seen everything the same, but
I felt him on that. And I'm feelin' him now, here with you.
Standin' in front of that rich, overfed, oblivious senate, I bet
Othello was feelin' his pop too; his pop who said, "Your
ancestors raised castles over all of Al-Andalus while the tribes
of Iberia squatted in the darkness of their own ignorance,
you don't take shit off a' nobody!" Ya see, for you, at best,

Othello is like your little exercise in understanding. You
think you get him like they think they get Nigger Jim; you
can commiserate, you have empathy for his condition. No
you do not. You have never had to, you will never have to.
And there is nothing more infuriating than white folks actin'
like they know your story well enough to tell it without your
help. Othello, whether he voiced it or not, would take issue
with you, Michael . . . And if I'm gonna do right by him,
every time I audition for this play is a conflict of interests.
He'll tolerate you because he wants the job; because
absurdly—to his horror—after ages, and generations, after
four hundred years he *still* finds himself beholden to the
likes of *you* for the opportunity to do the thing that he does
better than anything else he's ever done. So he'll take your
endless slights that you barely know you're offerin', your
hollow compliments—"Man, you're tall!" Gimme a fuckin'
break!!!—but he'll take it all, and he'll say, "Thank you."

> *He drives to the end of ALL he now*
> *cannot NOT say . . .*

Now me? Forgive me. But you have got an opportunity here.
This play? I don't advise it. But, if you must, and if anything
matters to you beyond what you think you know . . . Please
. . . put down your little brief authority, as you are certainly
most ignorant of what you are most assured, and talk with
me. Tell me what scares you, tell me what hurts you, tell
me what makes you aroused. Go deep. Engage me even
though you think it might be a huge mistake. Yes, have the
dauntlessness to challenge me with your beliefs, but also the
valor it takes to have those beliefs challenged. Stand up and
throw down, 'cuz I'm gonna. That's what I do. Mercenary
actors, mercenary soldiers, that's what we all do, and feel the
holy pleasure of God in the act. You have the courage not to
dismiss me, I believe in you, Michael. I know you do. Tell me
what you hate . . . what you fear. Trust me. I will protect you.
I will not let anything hurt you. Talk with me. We got so
much to talk about. We ain't gotten past Othello's first
speech and everything they told you is a lie. Commune with

me in contemplation of the magnitude of moment before
us. Honor it with something, anything more than simply
Brabantio's privilege of place. Meet me here, in this sacred
space, with *half* the courage of a Desdemona and I will lift
you, in life and love, in death and despair. I don't give a fuck
what English asshole you studied with, we will lift each other
and this *American* form. Hear me. See me . . . Three weeks
. . . my Brother. The clock is tickin' . . . God knows I ain't
easy . . . but no future worth the havin' ever was . . . If we're
gonna do this . . . let's do this . . .

> *This is a long, silent beat . . . In it,*
> *there hangs only every hope for the*
> *future . . .*

Director   . . . Thank you . . . Thanks for coming in.

> *The* **Actor** *absorbs this. He stands*
> *. . . ready to do we know not what. Is*
> *there that "hint of a recurring smile?"*

Actor   . . . Sure . . . Any time . . .

> *He stands . . .*

Fade to black.

Appendix

In writing about American race relations, the elements to be explored grow dense, complex, and tangential very quickly. In writing *American Moor*, the attempt to create the best play from that density required inevitably that elements be removed, not because they were irrelevant, but because they were not helpful in achieving the most focused and impactful dramatic arc. I here offer back a few of those elements. These pieces of text are excerpted from the play as it was performed for the Boston debut production at The Plaza Theatre, Boston Center for the Arts, July and August, 2017, produced by Phoenix Theatre Ensemble, and O.W.I. (Bureau of Theatre). I include them here *because* of their relevance to the experience of at least one African-American male actor, in the hope that they will be useful in the study and contemplation of this play and its themes as performance and as literature.

KHC

Appendix 1 (see p. 28)

They say of us, actors that is, who know that we are actors first and deeply, that we must harbor the most arrogant of hearts to presume that people would be compelled to sit and watch us with rapt attention upon a stage. But also, that we must harbor the most heroic of hearts in order to weather the endless rejection as we continue to venture forth,

> *The energy of this thought actually does pull him up out of the chair and onto his feet again.*

cleaving stalwartly to that sense of self; to seek distinction in an industry that perpetually tells us, "You are *not* compelling enough. You are *not* good enough. Everything about you is *wrong*." The same was said, and still is thought in no small corners of the collective American subconscious, of Black men and women who once presumed that they might rise above the station of common laborer and be of greater service to the world as physicians and attorneys. What then of Black actors presuming that *their* best service lives in lending as much to any aspect of the American acting tradition as any other American thespian, or English one, as no less seems the fucking ridiculous case?

I had long since ceased to be an English major. I was an eagerly aspiring American actor, in love with Shakespeare, and as such I was begrudgingly admitted into Shakespeare 101 in the College of Arts and Sciences at NYU, where I had come seeking to further expand the intellectual base that I, in my pursuits, would later spring from and land upon. You see, men of color can be quite rational too . . . Of my professor, proud, elder, learnèd, and white I thought the world. And the world in its wisdom did not for a moment question his scholarship or his prideful self-definition. However, my attraction to his strength of ego, taking the form of an ever eagerness to engage him on intricate points of textual analysis, he received as a challenge, which made

him irascible. But it gave me to wonder; to think, as a
troublesome actor too often will . . .

>   *As an annoyed, and over-eager*
>   *manchild of a student might ask . . .*

Who answered the questions of a childish upstart Arab-
Iberian soldier of fortune? And was he answered with
encouragement, or allowed his learning only grudgingly.
Either would have been an education. Both make us who
we become. We are never taught much. But we learn a
great deal.

So I got a "C" in Shakespeare 101 for English majors.
Holding a "B" average on all of the written work, I could
only assume that my professor rated his most engaged
student's in-class contributions no worthier than a "D." To
me, the grade said, "Mind your place." But hey, I'm an actor,
right? Overly dramatic, and sensitive . . . But it was the
pretty, big-breasted, red-headed coed who sat one desk
across who leaned over one day and whispered, "Psst . . . I
think he's scared of you a little bit."

> "*. . . which I observing,*
> *Took once a pliant hour, and found good means*
> *To draw from her a prayer of earnest heart*
> *That I would all my pilgrimage dilate . . .*"

I did consent. I mean, what was I gonna do, say "no?"

Yet one other thing that, as a young Moor, I was not taught,
but that I learned . . . Desdemona . . . Lovely, self-possessed,
listening, discerning, inconceivably brave, watching.
Desdemona is thrilled that such a man even exists. That one
of him is actually a thing is a joyous revelation to her. Her
very being emanates . . . upon seeing him standing there,
what is he, he's large, and dashing and dark, yeah sure
whatever, how he moves, like nothing she's ever seen, how
he stands, sure, fine. Look, so far beyond any of that bullshit
. . . is how, beneath a too often scowling brow poorly
concealing fifty years of adversity, she can see a child's eyes,

and a little boy's thoughts forming behind them, and how
his sculpted mouth makes words, and yet they are not
always the words that express the thoughts that she sees him
thinking . . . How far more often she sees that they are just
the things that his situation demands that he say. And as she
sits demurely through these congresses of men, her being in
silence exclaims, "For the fact that such as you so much as
breathes I am jubilant. I feel you deeply, great and lovely
thing, in my heart, and in my throat, and in my belly."

I had a Desdemona named Monica Greene. The things you
can do with a naked girl in that first flush of wanting just so
much to be done to by you . . . Mornings, she would cook
me matzah brei, ya know, the big crackers, cooked up in
scrambled eggs. And I would eat, noisily, like a ravenous old
. . . well, young black ram with my head in a trough. And
when, upon occasion, I would look up to see her gazing back
across the kitchen table at me, I would see reflected in her
adoring face, even with soft scrambled eggs dribbling down
my chin, a good and perfect personage whom the world
beyond her embrace would often make me to forget I knew
. . . Does Desdemona really want to be done to? Yeah . . . She
does. Why? Not because he tells really great stories . . . But
because he bears no scent of the pretense afforded the
privileged. As a Black boy, this American life has never been
my game to play. If I try to play it, my only strategy has ever
been to attempt to appear less of what I am. But this is a
fool's errand, because the thing that I am is so very
apparent, and really quite impossible to disguise. And so,
though I fit not your equation as seen through your narrow
little lens, little shall I grace my cause, Othello's cause, the
play's cause, the American theatre's cause, to pretend that I
don't know that you are frightened of me.

He returns to the chair and sits.

You are afraid of me. I am afraid that nothing will ever
change. And these are the forgeries of jealousy.

Appendix 2 (see p. 30)

Actor   Nobody ever plays the devil's advocate. They play their own advocate, and hide behind that stupid idiom to avoid having to take responsibility for it.

Director   You do get that, right?

Actor   Yes . . . And now that I've crucified my every chance of actually getting this gig, let's talk about one of the few things that you and I *both* know for a fact . . .

The period of time allotted for the rehearsal of a play in the American regional theatre is, as a general rule, no more than three weeks. Matters of money will not allow for longer. And in many cases, owing to these same financial concerns, that period has been condensed even further to two weeks, thus more or less assuring us of an exercise in mediocrity that audiences will, nonetheless, applaud because we have lost our perspective on excellence thereby causing them to lose theirs too. The bottom line? Your two weeks and change in the rehearsal hall is analogous to your five minutes lookin' at me in this room. Othello on the page, or the Black man in front of you; in that short space you can't do nothing but fucking pretend to know shit about either. Given that fact, why you wanna do *this* play?

> *Again, authentically the energy of his
> dissertation brings him to his feet.*

Why you wanna punish yourself with having some big-ass angry Negro all up in your grill getting ready to so ungently disabuse you of all of your most deeply seated notions about sex and race and religion, and most important, self? You ain't gonna confront those notions fully if you rehearse for a year, and you want to give it three weeks. Not to discover nothin' you ain't busy believin' already. How scary would that be? You wanna take what you think you know, and ram it greaseless into that three-week hole whether it fits or not and call it "theatre." Well, ouch!!

Appendix 3 (see p. 35)

Now, in his head, as he is facile in the assessing of any battle, he can reckon with ease what time and conditions hold in his favor and which do not. The stakes are high. There before the senate he fights, I think, the hint of a recurring smile. It's a smile that wants to say, "Ya gotta be kiddin' me with this shit, Senator. Ya want I should fight a war, or keep dickin' around with this clown over here?" Or, perhaps all it wants to say, just once, out loud, "Your precious little pink flower of feminine perfection chose me . . . And not only am I Black, I'm fuckin' fifty-two . . ."

> *He turns to make his way back to the chair, but he is struck by a sudden and sharp leg pain. Suddenly, not as sure on his feet, the chair seems a long way off, and people are watching. He hobbles slightly as if attempting to hide the old "war wound . . ." Maybe he hides several . . .*

But within, where we fortress up our more fragile selves . . .

> *He goes for the chair in one swift move, awkwardly covering the pain and effort for those observing, and he sits, relieved.*

He knows he is old . . . He knows he is epileptic . . . He knows by now that no one is going to erect a statue on the Rialto to the memory of the great General Othello, the Moor.

Methuen Drama Modern Plays

include work by

Bola Agbaje
Edward Albee
Davey Anderson
Jean Anouilh
John Arden
Peter Barnes
Sebastian Barry
Alistair Beaton
Brendan Behan
Edward Bond
William Boyd
Bertolt Brecht
Howard Brenton
Amelia Bullmore
Anthony Burgess
Leo Butler
Jim Cartwright
Lolita Chakrabarti
Caryl Churchill
Lucinda Coxon
Curious Directive
Nick Darke
Shelagh Delaney
Ishy Din
Claire Dowie
David Edgar
David Eldridge
Dario Fo
Michael Frayn
John Godber
Paul Godfrey
James Graham
David Greig
John Guare
Mark Haddon
Peter Handke
David Harrower
Jonathan Harvey
Iain Heggie

Robert Holman
Caroline Horton
Terry Johnson
Sarah Kane
Barrie Keeffe
Doug Lucie
Anders Lustgarten
David Mamet
Patrick Marber
Martin McDonagh
Arthur Miller
D. C. Moore
Tom Murphy
Phyllis Nagy
Anthony Neilson
Peter Nichols
Joe Orton
Joe Penhall
Luigi Pirandello
Stephen Poliakoff
Lucy Prebble
Peter Quilter
Mark Ravenhill
Philip Ridley
Willy Russell
Jean-Paul Sartre
Sam Shepard
Martin Sherman
Wole Soyinka
Simon Stephens
Peter Straughan
Kate Tempest
Theatre Workshop
Judy Upton
Timberlake Wertenbaker
Roy Williams
Snoo Wilson
Frances Ya-Chu Cowhig
Benjamin Zephaniah

Methuen Drama Contemporary Dramatists

include

John Arden (two volumes)
Arden & D'Arcy
Peter Barnes (three volumes)
Sebastian Barry
Mike Bartlett
Dermot Bolger
Edward Bond (ten volumes)
Howard Brenton (two volumes)
Leo Butler (two volumes)
Richard Cameron
Jim Cartwright
Caryl Churchill (two volumes)
Complicite
Sarah Daniels (two volumes)
Nick Darke
David Edgar (three volumes)
David Eldridge (two volumes)
Ben Elton
Per Olov Enquist
Dario Fo (two volumes)
Michael Frayn (four volumes)
John Godber (four volumes)
Paul Godfrey
James Graham (two volumes)
David Greig
John Guare
Lee Hall (two volumes)
Katori Hall
Peter Handke
Jonathan Harvey (two volumes)
Iain Heggie
Israel Horovitz
Declan Hughes
Terry Johnson (three volumes)
Sarah Kane
Barrie Keeffe
Bernard-Marie Koltès (two volumes)
Franz Xaver Kroetz
Kwame Kwei-Armah
David Lan
Bryony Lavery
Deborah Levy
Doug Lucie

David Mamet (four volumes)
Patrick Marber
Martin McDonagh
Duncan McLean
David Mercer (two volumes)
Anthony Minghella (two volumes)
Tom Murphy (six volumes)
Phyllis Nagy
Anthony Neilson (two volumes)
Peter Nichol (two volumes)
Philip Osment
Gary Owen
Louise Page
Stewart Parker (two volumes)
Joe Penhall (two volumes)
Stephen Poliakoff (three volumes)
David Rabe (two volumes)
Mark Ravenhill (three volumes)
Christina Reid
Philip Ridley (two volumes)
Willy Russell
Eric-Emmanuel Schmitt
Ntozake Shange
Sam Shepard (two volumes)
Martin Sherman (two volumes)
Christopher Shinn (two volumes)
Joshua Sobel
Wole Soyinka (two volumes)
Simon Stephens (three volumes)
Shelagh Stephenson
David Storey (three volumes)
C. P. Taylor
Sue Townsend
Judy Upton
Michel Vinaver (two volumes)
Arnold Wesker (two volumes)
Peter Whelan
Michael Wilcox
Roy Williams (four volumes)
David Williamson
Snoo Wilson (two volumes)
David Wood (two volumes)
Victoria Wood

Bloomsbury Methuen Drama World Classics

include

Jean Anouilh (two volumes)
Brendan Behan
Aphra Behn
Bertolt Brecht (eight volumes)
Büchner
Bulgakov
Calderón
Čapek
Anton Chekhov
Noël Coward (eight volumes)
Feydeau
Eduardo De Filippo
Max Frisch
John Galsworthy
Gogol
Gorky (two volumes)
Harley Granville Barker
  (two volumes)
Victor Hugo
Henrik Ibsen (six volumes)
Jarry

Lorca (three volumes)
Marivaux
Mustapha Matura
David Mercer (two volumes)
Arthur Miller (five volumes)
Molière
Musset
Peter Nichols (two volumes)
Joe Orton
A. W. Pinero
Luigi Pirandello
Terence Rattigan
  (two volumes)
W. Somerset Maugham
  (two volumes)
August Strindberg
  (three volumes)
J. M. Synge
Ramón del Valle-Inclan
Frank Wedekind
Oscar Wilde

For a complete listing of
Methuen Drama titles, visit:
www.bloomsbury.com/drama

Follow us on Twitter and keep up to date
with our news and publications
@MethuenDrama